CAPE EDITIONS 43

How are
Verses Made?
Vladimir
Mayakovsky

Translated from the Russian by G. M. Hyde

JONATHAN CAPE
THIRTY BEDFORD SQUARE
LONDON

First published in 1926 in the U.S.S.R. under the title
Kak delat' stikhi?
This translation first published 1970
English translation and Introduction © 1970 by G. M. Hyde
Jonathan Cape Ltd, 30 Bedford Square, London wc1

SBN Paperback edition 224 61896 2
      Hardback edition 224 61895 4

Printed and bound in Great Britain
by Richard Clay (The Chaucer Press), Ltd
Bungay, Suffolk

Contents

INTRODUCTORY NOTE

Vladimir Vladimirovich Mayakovsky, arguably the greatest Soviet poet, was born in Bagdadi (now Mayakovsky), Georgia, in 1883, and shot himself in Moscow in 1930. The son of a forester, he was an active revolutionary very early in his life, and when revolution at last came to Russia in 1917, Mayakovsky claimed it as his own. A highly sensitive and very vulnerable man, he dedicated his talents utterly to the Soviet cause, adopting a public voice, and declaring in one of his poems ('Homewards', 1925)

> I want
>   the State Planning Authority
>   to sweat,
>   Debating my quota for the year.

The present essay (written in 1926; for a brief account of its genesis, see n 5) represents Mayakovsky's attempt to formulate a new and thoroughly Socialist aesthetics: to sustain the experimental and innovatory impetus of the Futurist movement while rejecting its Bohemianism. The creative process in the expanded metaphor of *How are verses made?* is assimilated to the productive processes of the new Socialist economy, without any of the crude yoking together of literature and politics that damages some later Soviet literary criticism and theory; and Mayakovsky enlists the delicate analytical techniques of the Formalist critics to his own urgent preoccupation with history, without blunting his critical instruments. At the same time in neutralizing the sentimental individualism of Esenin's farewell poem (see Ch. 2, n 61), and the illegitimate use that was made of it, Mayakovsky has given us a permanently challenging account of the poet's responsibility to the people; the language of poetry or of critical discourse is for him, in Hopkins's formulation, truly the 'current language heightened'.

Stalin's canonization of Mayakovsky ('He was, and is, the greatest poet of our Socialist epoch.') was described by Pasternak as 'his second death'. His first has been accounted for in terms of the growing dogmatism in the intellectual life of the time, but probably has as much to do with Mayakovsky's personal instability: his relationship with Lily Brik, the subject of his major poem 'About This', lasted from the time he met Lily and her husband Osip Brik, in 1915, until his death, without ever becoming clear. In addition he was at the time of his death deeply involved with a Russian emigrée in Paris, whom he was precluded from visiting by the growing restrictions on foreign travel. His last, unfinished poem 'At the Top of my Voice' conveys a sense of agonizing disjunction between his personal anguish and confusion and the social responsibilities that his art had taken upon itself.

University of East Anglia
1970   G. M. HYDE

ACKNOWLEDGMENTS

I am extremely grateful to Mr Stanley Mitchell, of the University of Essex, for his help in checking my translation and for making several very valuable suggestions.

I should also like to acknowledge a debt to the German translation of Hugo Huppert, and the abridged French translation of Elsa Triolet, to which I made frequent reference.

The text is taken from the *Complete Works* published in Moscow, 1939–49 (see Bibliography).

HOW ARE VERSES MADE?

Vladimir Mayakovsky

I.

I have to write on this subject.

In different literary debates, in conversations with young workers from various workshops of the word (Rapp, Tapp, Papp, etc.),[1] in reprisals against critics, I have often been obliged, if not to smash to pieces, at least to discredit the old poetics. Of course we didn't interfere with old poetry that was in itself quite blameless. It drew our wrath only if avid protectors of the old hid from new art behind the backsides of monuments.

Quite the reverse – removing, shaking up, and overturning monuments, we showed our readers what the Great looked like from a completely unknown, unexplored viewpoint.

Children (and young literary schools as well) are always curious to know what is inside a cardboard horse. After the work of the Formalists[2] the insides of cardboard horses and elephants stand revealed. If the horse is a bit spoiled because of this – so sorry! We mustn't squabble with the poetry of the past – it provides us with a textbook to study.

Our chief and enduring hatred falls on sentimental-critical Philistinism. On those who see all the greatness of the poetry of the past in the fact that they too have loved as Oniegin loved Tatyana[3] (elective affinities!) or in the fact that even they can understand these poets (they studied them at school), and iambuses caress *their* ears too. This facile Black Mass is hateful to us because it casts around difficult and important poetical work an atmosphere of sexual trembles and palpitations, in which one believes that only eternal poetry is safe from the dialectical process, and the only method of production is the inspired throwing back of the head while one waits for the heavenly soul of poetry to descend on one's bald patch in the form of a dove, a peacock or an ostrich.

It isn't difficult to unmask these gentlemen.

All you have to do is compare Tatyana's love and 'the science of which Ovid sang' with a programme of legislation about marriage, read about Pushkin's 'superior, disenchanted lorgnette' to the Donets coal miners, or run in front of the May-day processions declaiming 'My uncle showed his good intentions ...'[4]

After an experiment like that, I hardly think any young man, burning to give his energies to the Revolution, will feel any great urge to spend time studying ancient poetic skills.

A lot has been said and written about this. The noisy acclaim of the public halls was always on our side. But straight after the acclaim sceptical voices were raised:

'You only destroy, you create nothing!' 'The old textbooks were bad, but where are the new ones?' 'Give us the *rules* of your poetics!' 'Give us textbooks!'

To plead that the old poetics has lasted fifteen hundred years, and ours thirty, doesn't help much.

Do you want to write, and want to know how it's done? Why do they refuse to accept as poetry something that's written according to all Shengeli's rules, with rich rhymes, iambuses and trochees? You're right to demand of poets that they shouldn't carry with them to the grave the secrets of their skill.

I want to write about poetry not as a pedant, but as a practitioner. My article has no scholarly signifi-

12

cance. I write about my work, which, by the light of my observations and convictions, I see as differing very little from the work of other professional poets.

Once again I want to insist that I offer no rules to make anyone a poet, by following which he can write poetry. Such rules simply don't exist. A poet is a person who creates these very rules.

For the hundredth time I offer my tired old example and analogy.

A mathematician is a man who establishes, enlarges, and develops mathematical rules, a man who introduces new concepts into mathematical knowledge. The man who first formulated the proposition that 'Two and two are four' was a great mathematician, even if he arrived at this truth by putting together two butt-ends with two more butt-ends. Everyone who came after him, even if they put together incomparably bigger things – a railway-engine with a railway-engine, for example – all these people are not mathematicians. This assertion doesn't at all belittle the work of a man who puts railway-engines together. His work, when transport is in chaos, can be a hundred times more valuable than a bare arithmetical truth. But you mustn't send a handbook on repairing railway-engines to a Mathematical Society and demand that it should rank with the geometry of Lobachevsky.[6] This will enrage the planning commission, puzzle the mathematicians and nonplus the Tariff Committee.

They'll tell me that I'm labouring to explain the obvious, that all this is quite clear. Nothing of the kind.

Eighty per cent of the rhymed rubbish that is printed by our publishers gets published either because the editors have no notion of the poetry of the past, or don't know what poetry is for.

The editors know only 'I like it' or 'I don't like it',

forgetting that taste, too, can and must be developed. Almost all editors complain to me that they don't know how to turn away a poetry manuscript, they don't know what to say about it.

A literate editor should have said to the poet: 'Your verses are very correct, they are composed according to the third edition of Brodovsky's handbook, or Shengeli's, or Grech's, and so on and so forth; all your rhymes are well-tried rhymes, long ago included in V. Abramov's complete dictionary of Russian rhymes.[7] Since at the moment I haven't got any good poems, I'll willingly take yours, paying for them, as the work of a qualified copyist, at the rate of three roubles a sheet, on condition that you provide three copies.'

The poet has no let-out. Either he stops writing, or he sets to writing poetry as to a job that needs more work. In any case the poet gives up putting on airs in front of a working journalist, to whom even the latest news is worth only three roubles a paragraph. Our journalist, you see, was weaned on scandals and fires, but a poet of this type just wets his fingers and riffles through books.

In the name of raising the qualifications of poets, in the name of the future blossoming of poetry, we must expunge the idea that such facile undertakings should stand apart from other aspects of human endeavour.

I make this reservation: establishing rules is not in itself the aim of poetry, otherwise the poet turns into a scholar exercising his powers in formulating rules for non-existent or useless things and propositions. For example, it wouldn't be much use to make up a rule about how to count the stars while riding a bicycle.

A proposition which demands formulation, demands *rules*, is thrust upon us by life. Methods of ormulation, the aim of the rules, are defined by class and the needs of our struggle.

The Revolution, for instance, has thrown up on to the streets the unpolished speech of the masses, the slang of the suburbs has flowed along the downtown boulevards; the enfeebled sub-language of the intelligentsia, with its emasculated words 'ideal', 'principles of justice', 'the transcendental visage of Christ and Antichrist' – all these expressions, pronounced in little whispers in restaurants, have been trampled underfoot. There is a new linguistic element. How can one make it poetic? The old rules about 'love and dove', 'moon and June' and alexandrines are no use. How can we introduce the spoken language into poetry, and extract poetry from this spoken language?

Spit on the Revolution in the name of the iambus?

> Evil we've turned, become submissive too,
> We can't escape.
> Already led on predetermined tracks
> By blackened hands.
>
> (Z. Gippius)[8]

No!
It's hopeless to shove the bursting thunder of the Revolution into a four-stress amphibrach, devised for its gentle sound!

> O heroes, o sailors of seas, albatrosses,
> Guests at the tables of thunderous feasts.
> O great tribe of eagles, o sailors, o sailors,
> Ruby the flames of my song made for you.
>
> (Kirillov)[9]

No!
Or give full rights of citizenship straight away to

15

the new language: a scream instead of a refrain, the
rattle of a drum instead of a cradle song!

> Keep step with the revolution!
>
> (Blok)

> Deploy yourselves on the march!
>
> (Mayakovsky)*

It's not enough to give examples of the new poetry
the rules of how a word should act on the revolu
tionary masses – one must ensure that these word
will act in such a way as to give maximum suppor
to one's class.

It's not enough to say that the 'tireless enemy neve
sleeps'. (Blok)[12] You must show exactly or at leas
suggest unmistakably to the imagination what the
enemy looks like.

It's not enough to muster your forces and march
You must deploy yourself in accordance with all the
rules of street fighting, securing the post office, the
banks and the arsenals, in the hands of the revolu
tionary workers.

And so:

> Eat pineapples
> Guzzle grouse
> Your last day draws near, bourgeois ...
>
> (Mayakovsky)*

Classical poetry would hardly have permitted verse
like that. Grech in 1820 didn't know any *chas
tushky*,[14] but if he had known them he would have
written about them, I'm sure, in the same scornfu
tone in which he talks of popular versification
'These verses know nothing of metrical feet o
harmony.'

But the Petersburg streets fathered these lines. Critics can investigate at leisure what rules underlie them.

Neologisms are obligatory in writing poetry. The material of words and phrases that falls to the poet must be worked over. If old scraps of words present themselves in the composition of a poem, they must be in strict measure with the quantities of new material. Alloys of this kind are useful or not according to the quantity and quality of the new material in them.

Innovation, of course, doesn't posit the constant utterance of undreamed-of truths. The iambus, free verse, alliteration, assonance aren't invented every day. Work can be done on them, too, extending, going deeper, spreading wider in application.

'Twice two is four' – it doesn't live on its own, and it can't. You must know how to apply this truth (rules of application). You must make it memorable (more rules). You must show that it is irrefutable with a wealth of illustrative facts (example, content, theme).

From this it is clear that the depiction and representation of reality have no place in poetry on their own account. Work of that kind is necessary, but it must be evaluated as if it were the work of the secretary of a mass-meeting. It's just a matter of 'They listened, they made resolutions.' That's the tragedy of the fellow-travellers:[15] they heard five years ago and made their proposals a bit late – when all the rest had already put them into action.

Poetry is at its very root tendentious.

In my opinion, the line: 'I walk alone into the road'[16] constitutes agitation; the poet agitates for girls to walk with him. It's boring, you see, on your own! Ah, if only there were poetry as powerful as this calling people together into co-operatives!

The old textbooks on writing poetry, of course, weren't like that. They describe only a historical and already accepted mode of writing. Actually these books shouldn't be called 'how to write'[17] but 'how they used to write'.

I'll be honest with you. I know nothing of iambuses or trochees, I've never differentiated between them and I never will. Not because it's hard work, but because in my work I've had no occasion to concern myself with such things. And if snatches of such metres can be found, they've been written entirely by ear, because these time-worn patterns are encountered extraordinarily frequently ... like 'Down mother Volga's mighty stream'.

I've several times got down to studying this, understood the mechanics of it, and then forgotten again. Things like this, which take up ninety per cent of poetry textbooks, are about three per cent of my practical work!

In poetical work there are only a few general rules about how to begin. And these rules are a pure convention. Like in chess. The first moves are almost always the same. But already from the next move you begin to think up a new attack. The most inspired move can't be repeated in any given situation in your next game. Only its unexpectedness defeats the opponent.

Just like the unexpected rhymes in poetry.

What basic propositions are indispensable, when one begins poetical work?

First thing. The presence of a problem in society the solution of which is conceivable only in poetical terms. A social command. (An interesting theme for special study would be the disparity between the social command and actual commissions.)

Second thing. An exact knowledge, or rather intuition, of the desires of your class (or the group you
18

represent) on the question, i.e. a standpoint from which to take aim.

Third thing. Materials. Words. Fill your storehouse constantly, fill the granaries of your skull with all kinds of words, necessary, expressive, rare, invented, renovated and manufactured.

Fourth thing. Equipment for the plant and tools for the assembly line. A pen, a pencil, a typewriter, a telephone, an outfit for your visits to the doss-house, a bicycle for your trips to the publishers, a table in good order, an umbrella for writing in the rain, a room measuring the exact number of paces you have to take when you're working, connection with a press agency to send you information on questions of concern to the provinces and so on and so forth, and even a pipe and cigarettes.

Fifth thing. Skills and techniques of handling words, extremely personal things, which come only with years of daily work: rhymes, metres, alliteration, images, lowering of style, pathos, closure, finding a title, layout, and so on and so forth.

For example: the social task may be to provide the words for a song for the Red Army men on their way to the Petersburg front. The purpose is to defeat Yudenich.[18] The material is words from the vocabulary of soldiers. The tools of production – a pencil stub. The device – the rhymed *chastushka*.

The result:

> My darling gave me a long felt cloak
> And a pair of woolly socks.
> Yudenich scurries from Petersburg
> Fast as a smoked-out fox.

The originality of the quatrain, warranting the production of this *chastushka*, lies in the rhyming of 'woolly socks' and 'smoked-out fox'. It's this novelty that makes the thing relevant, poetical, and typical.

The effect of the *chastushka* depends on the device of unexpected rhymes where there is disharmony between the first pair of lines and the second. Thus the first two lines can be called subsidiary, or auxiliary.

Even these general and basic rules of poetic practice offer greater possibilities than we now have for labelling and classifying poetic works.

Aspects of the material used, the means of production and the technical skills can simply be regarded as quantifiable on a points system.

Did society demand this? It did. Two points. Is there an aim or purpose? Two points. Is it rhymed? Another point. Is there alliteration? Another half-point. And another point for the rhythm – since the strange measure necessitated bus journeys.

Let the critics smile, but I would rate the poetry of any Alaskan poet (other things being equal of course) higher than, let's say, the work of a poet from Yalta.

Well of course! The Alaskan must freeze, and buy a fur coat, and his ink solidifies in his fountain-pen. Whereas the Yalta poet writes against a background of palm trees, in surroundings which are nice even without poems.

Clear-sightedness about such matters is a component of a writer's qualifications.

The poetry of Demyan Bedny[19] presents an example of a social command for today which has been properly understood, an accurate sense of aim or purpose – the needs of the workers and the peasants – the vocabulary of a semi-peasant environment (with a dash of moribund poetical rhymes) and devices drawn from folklore.

The poetry of Kruchënikh:[20] alliteration, dissonance; its aim or purpose is to assist future poets.

Here there is no call to take up the metaphysical

20

question of who is better, Demyan Bedny or Kruch-enikh. These are poetical achievements of very different kinds, on different planes, and each of them can exist without excluding the other and without competing with the other.

As I see it, the fine poetical work would be one written to the social command of the Comintern,[21] taking for its purpose the victory of the proletariat, making its points in a new vocabulary, striking and comprehensible to all, fashioned on a table that is N.O.T.[22] equipment and sent to the publisher by plane. I insist, 'by plane', since the engagement of poetry with contemporary life is one of the most important factors in our production. Of course, the process of weighing up and evaluating poetry is subtler and more complex than I have suggested.

I am deliberately exaggerating, simplifying, and distorting my ideas. I am exaggerating because I want to show more strikingly that the essence of modern literary work doesn't lie in the evaluation of this or that ready-made thing from the standpoint of literary taste, but in a correct approach to the study of the productive process itself.

Far from being unconcerned with the evaluation of accepted images or devices, this article is concerned with an attempt to uncover the very process of poetic production.

How are verses made?

Work begins long before one receives or is aware of a social command.

Preliminary work goes on incessantly.

You can produce good poetic work to order only when you've a large stock of preliminaries behind you.

For example, at the moment (to write of what has this very minute come into my head) a fine surname, 'Mr Glyceron', is hammering away in my brain,

21

arriving quite by chance out of some garbled conversation about glycerine.

And some fine rhymes:

> In the creamy cloud masses
> Rose a grim fortress

> Go to Rome, France, or Germany,
> Find a refuge for a Bohemian.

> On a snorting mare
> I'll ride to the Amur,
> The Amur
> Mourns.

Or:

> Dense summer greenery ...
> August's rich finery etc., etc.

There's also the metre of an American song I like a lot, which needs to be adapted and Russified:

> Hard-hearted Hannah
> The vamp of Savannah
> The vamp of Savannah
> Gee-ay.

There's the tersely striking alliteration of a poster glimpsed in passing, with the name 'Flora Low':

> Where can I find Flora Low?
> Flora's on the lower floor.

Or, in connection with a synthetic dye factory, called Lyamina's:

> Mummy mixes lovely dye
> 'Cos my mummy's Lyamina.

There are themes of varying clarity and obscurity:
1. Rain in New York.
2. A prostitute on the Boulevard des Capucines in Paris. A prostitute who's considered very smart to sleep with because she's only got one leg – the other one, it seems, was cut off by a tram.
3. An old man in the lavatory of the Hessler restaurant in Berlin.
4. The great theme of the Revolution, which couldn't be done unless you'd lived through it in a village. And so on and so forth.

All these preliminaries are put together in one's head, and the most difficult ones are noted down.

The manner of their future application is all obscure to me, but I know they will be made use of.

All my time goes on these preliminaries. I spend from ten to eighteen hours each day on them, and I'm almost always muttering something or other. My concentration on them accounts for my notorious poetic absent-mindedness.

Work on them goes on with such intensity that in ninety cases out of a hundred I even know the very place where, in all that fifteen years of work, such-and-such a rhyme, alliteration or image came to me and took on its final shape.

> A street.
> I meet ... (The tram from the Sukharev tower to the Sretenka gate, 1913)
>
> A menacing rain narrowed the eyes,
> While I ... (The Strastnoy monastery, 1912)
>
> Stroke the shrivelled black cats (Oak tree in Kuntsevo, 1914)

Left
Left. (Cab on the Embankment, 1917)

D'Anthèse, son of a bitch. (In the train near Mytishchi, 1924)

And so on and so forth.

This 'notebook' is one of the most important pre conditions for the composition of the genuine article.

People usually only write about this little book after the poet's death; for years it lies gathering dust, and it's printed posthumously, long after the 'finished' works, but for the writer this book is all in-all.

Inexperienced poets naturally lack this little book since they lack practice and experience. Properly worked-out lines are few, and that's why their whole output is anaemic and tedious.

No beginner will, whatever his talents, write something fine straight off; on the other hand, first work is always 'fresher', since it is a vehicle for the stored-up impressions of the time that preceded it.

Only the presence of rigorously thought-out pre liminary work gives me the time to finish anything, since my normal output of work in progress is eight to ten lines a day.

A poet regards every meeting, every signpost, every event in whatever circumstances simply as material to be shaped into words.

Once upon a time I embarked on such work as if fearful even to utter words and expressions that seemed to me needful for future poems – I became gloomy, dull and untalkative.

In about 1913, when I was returning from Saratov to Moscow, so as to prove my devotion to a certain female companion, I told her that I was 'not a man

but a cloud in trousers'. When I'd said it, I immediately thought it could be used in a poem; but
what if it should at once circulate in conversation
and be squandered to no avail? Terribly worried, I
put leading questions to the girl for half an hour, and
calmed down only when I was quite sure that my
words were going in one ear and out the other.

Two years later I needed 'a cloud in trousers' for
the title of a whole long poem.

For two days I pondered words to describe the
tenderness a lonely man feels for his only love.

How will he cherish and love her?

On the third night I went to bed with a headache,
and hadn't thought up anything. During the night the
formulation came:

> Your body
> I shall cherish and love
> As a soldier
> Crippled by war
> Useless
> Belonging to no one
> Cherishes his one leg.[23]

I leapt out of bed half-awake. By the dim light of
a burnt-down match I wrote on a cigarette packet
'his one leg' and went to sleep. In the morning I
puzzled for about two hours over that 'his one leg'
written on my cigarette packet; I wondered how it
had got there.

A rhyme that has been hooked but not yet landed
can poison one's whole existence: you talk without
knowing what you're saying, in a daze, you don't
sleep, you can almost see that rhyme flying past
your eyes.

Our present-day Shengelis have begun to handle
poetical work with his contemptuous adroitness, as

if it were the merest trifle. There are even fine young lads who outdo their teacher. Here, for instance, is an advert from the Kharkov *Proletarian* (No. 256):

'How do you become a writer?

Send 50 kopecks in stamps for details. Slavyansk, on the Donets railway, Box number 11.'

Handy, isn't it?!

By the way, this is a product of the pre-revolutionary period. Like the supplement enclosed in the journal *Divertissement*,[24] a little book called *How to be a Poet in Five Easy Lessons*.

I believe that even my brief examples will put poetry where it truly belongs, among the most difficult and laborious jobs.

One's attitude to the stanza must be like the attitude to the woman in Pasternak's inspired quatrain:

> Like some provincial Shakespearian actor
> I wandered with you, repeating my part.
> From head to foot, I knew you by heart
> That day, your ways and your graces.[25]

In the next chapter I shall try to show how a poem grows from these preliminaries, by means of concrete reference to one of my own poems.

2.

The most effective of my recent poems is, in my opinion, 'To Sergey Esenin.'

I didn't have to look for a paper to print it or a publisher – they circulated it in copies before publication, secretly made off with it from the printer's and published it in a provincial newspaper; my audience actually demanded to hear it read, and during the reading you could have heard a pin drop; afterwards people came up to me, wringing their paws with emotion, in the corridors they raged or eulogized, and on the day it was published the review was a mixture of curses and compliments.

How was this poem produced?

I had known Esenin for a long time – ten or twelve years.

When I first met him he was wearing his bast shoes and his peasant shirt with some sort of little crosses sewn on to it. This was in one of the best flats in Leningrad. Knowing how delighted a real peasant (as opposed to an ornamental one) is to swap his outfit for a pair of boots and a jacket, I didn't quite trust Esenin. He seemed to me a bit operatic, or like a tailor's dummy. The more so since he had already written poetry which had been well received, and could certainly have found the cash for a pair of boots.

As a man who has in his time worn – and left off wearing – a yellow Futurist jacket, I made business-like inquiries about these clothes.

'What's this, an advertising stunt?'

Esenin answered me in a voice like icon-lamp oil come to life.

Something like:

'We rustic folk, we know nothing of these queer ways of yours ... we have what you might call ... our own ... age-old, pastoral ...'

His own very talented and very rustic verses were of course anathema to us Futurists.

But just the same he was a nice, amusing sort of chap.

On parting, I said casually:

'I bet you'll give up those bast shoes and the whole coxcombry!'

Esenin retorted with righteous warmth. Kluyev[1] led him aside like a mother appropriating her flighty daughter, when she's afraid the daughter hasn't the

27

strength or the inclination to stand up for herself.

Another glimpse of Esenin. I met him again in the flesh after the Revolution at Gorky's place.[2] At once, with the full force of my inborn tactlessness, I yelled:

'I win the bet, Esenin, you're wearing a jacket and a tie!'

Esenin got very angry and went to work it out on someone else.

Then I kept coming across lines of Esenin's which I couldn't help liking, such as:

> My dear, dear ridiculous clown ... etc.
> The sky is a bell, its clapper the moon ... etc.

Esenin cut loose from his mythical idealized village, but cut loose, of course, with some relapses, and together with

> My darling mother country
> I am a Bolshevik ...

appeared poems extolling cows. Instead of a memorial to Marx, what he wanted was a cow memorial. Not the sort of cow that yields milk, but a cowy symbol, with its horns pushing against a railway-engine.

We often crossed swords with Esenin, holding him responsible for all the Imaginists who grew up in rank profusion around him.

Then Esenin went off to America and other places and came back with a marked yearning for something new.

Unfortunately, at this period one came across him more often in police records than in poetry. He rapidly and unhesitatingly left the ranks of the healthy workers in verse. (I speak of that minimal health that's required of a poet.)

At this time I met Esenin on a few occasions, and

28

he meetings were lyrical, without the least discord.

I watched with pleasure as Esenin evolved from imaginism[3] to the V.A.P.P.[4] He spoke with interest of the work of others. This was one new trait in Esenin (who loved himself inordinately): he was rather envious of any poet who had become organically one with the Revolution and the proletariat, and who saw a great and hopeful road leading on.

This, in my opinion, is the basis of Esenin's poetic irritability and his dissatisfaction with himself, manifesting itself in his wine-drinking and his brusque and maladroit relations with those around him.

In his final days Esenin even showed some evident sympathy for us, the LEF group: he would call on Aseyev,[5] ring me up, or sometimes simply tried to drop in on us.

He got a bit podgy and flabby, but remained elegant in the Esenin manner.

My last meeting with him produced on me a painful and unforgettable impression. In the cashier's office at the State Publishing House I met a man who came rushing towards me, his face swollen, his tie crooked, and wearing a hat which kept in place quite by chance, clinging to his corn-coloured locks. From him and his two dubious (to me, at all events) companions I caught a whiff of spirits. I literally had difficulty in recognizing Esenin. It was a problem to turn aside the demand that soon followed, that I should go and drink with him, backed up by much waving of thick wads of ten-rouble notes, and all day kept calling to mind this painful scene. In the evening, of course, I had long talks (alas, no one ever does more than talk in these situations) with colleagues, about how we must do something for Esenin. They and I cursed his 'milieu' and we went away persuading ourselves that his friends the Eseninists would look after him.

That wasn't how it turned out. Esenin's end was
saddening, as such things humanly are. But it seemed
all at once entirely natural and logical. I heard the
news at night; my grief, however sincere, would have
lessened by morning, but in the morning the newspapers carried his suicide poem:

> In this life to die is nothing new
> But to live, of course, is nothing newer ...

After these lines Esenin's death became a literary
fact.[6]

It was at once clear how many insecure people
these powerful lines, just these very lines of poetry
could bring to the rope or the revolver.

And no amount of analysis in the newspapers, no
amount of articles, can wipe out these lines.

One can and must combat these verses only with
verses.

In this way society demanded that Soviet poets
should write a poem about Esenin. The command
was unusually important and urgent, since Esenin's
lines had rapidly and inexorably begun to act. Many
poets accepted the command. But what could one
write? and how?

Poems appeared, articles, reminiscences, essays and
even plays. In my opinion, ninety-nine per cent of
everything written about Esenin is simply rubbish, or
lying rubbish.

The poems by Esenin's friends are piffle. You can
easily recognize them by their attitude to Esenin:
they address him like one of the family, as 'Seryozha'
(which is how Bezimensky[7] got hold of this unsuitable word). 'Seryozha' doesn't exist as a literary fact.
There is a poet – Sergey Esenin. Please let's talk about
him. Use of the familiar 'Seryozha' immediately
short-circuits the social command and efforts to

30

'ormulate it. That word '*Seryozha*' reduces a huge and complex topic to the level of an epigram or a chanson. And all the tears of the poetic relatives of the deceased don't help in the least. Such verses can't do the job of poetry. Poetry like this only moves us to laughter or irritation.

The poems of Esenin's 'enemies', even though these men have been placated by his death, are all Pharisaical. They refuse Esenin a poetic burial simply because of the fact of his suicide.

> But miserable hooliganism like this
> We never expected, even from you
> (Zharov, I think)[8]

The poetry of these men is the poetry of a hastily implemented but poorly understood social command, and in it notions of aim or purpose are totally unconnected with the methods employed. The result is a low journalistic style quite ineffectual on this tragic occasion.

A suicide torn from its complex social and psychological context, ascribed to a momentary unmotivated act of negation (how else could it appear?!) is a saddeningly false picture.

Nor is the prose about him any more use in combating the latest pernicious Eseninist poems.

It begins with Kogan,[9] who, it seems to me, didn't learn his Marxism from Marx, but tried to derive it unaided from the dictum of Gorky's Luka[10] – 'fleas aren't so bad, little black hopping things' – considering this truth to be highly scientific and objective and therefore, in Esenin's absence (posthumously), writing an encomiastic article that is no use to man or beast; and ends with the stinking little books of Kruchënikh,[11] who teaches Esenin the rudiments of politics as though Kruchënikh had himself spent all his life

31

doing hard labour, struggling for freedom, and a
though it had cost him a huge effort to write six(!
booklets about Esenin with a hand still raw from th
jangling manacles.

So what can we write about Esenin, and how?

After considering his death from all angles, an
leafing through a lot of unfamiliar material, I formu
lated the problem and put it to myself.

Aim or purpose: deliberately to neutralize th
effect of Esenin's last lines, to make Esenin's deat
uninteresting, to replace the facile beauty of death b
another beauty, since toiling mankind needs all it
strength to sustain the Revolution it has begun; re
gardless of the obstacles on the way, the strenuou
contradictions of the New Economic Policy;[12] it re
quires us to pay tribute to life's happiness, the joy o
this enormously difficult advance towards Com
munism.

At this moment, having the poem to hand, it's easy
to formulate, but how difficult it was then to begi
writing!

The work happened to coincide with my excur
sions to the provinces and public lectures. For abou
three months I came back day after day to my sub
ject and could think of nothing sensible. All kind
of diabolic nonsense sprang to mind, little devils wit
blue faces and snouts like water-pipes. For thre
months I couldn't think of a single line. From th
daily sifting of words only a few beginnings of rhyme
were winnowed out, such as 'hubbub – pub', 'Koga
– rogue', 'Napostov[13] – more than enough'. When
was already on my way back to Moscow I realize
that my difficulties and my slowness in writing wer
the result of too close a correspondence between m
own circumstances and those I was writing about.

The same hotel rooms, the same water-pipes, th
same enforced solitude.

32

These surroundings wound me into themselves, they wouldn't let me escape, they refused me the feelings and words I needed in order to brand and negate, they gave me no material from which I could educe sane and healthy impulses.

Whence comes what is almost a rule: to do anything poetic you positively need a change of place or of time.

Just as, for example, in painting, when you're drawing some object or other you have to stand back, at a distance equal to three times the size of the object. If you don't do that, you simply won't see the thing you're depicting.

The bigger the thing or the event, the further you have to get away from it. Feeble people mark time, and wait for whatever it is to pass by, so they can describe it, but the strong run forward just far enough to seize the event and draw it towards them.

Any description of contemporary events by those taking part in the struggles of the day will always be incomplete, even incorrect, or at any rate one-sided.

Evidently, work of this kind is a summation, the result of two different endeavours – the records of a contemporary, and a future artist's efforts to work outwards from such descriptions.

Herein lies the tragedy of the revolutionary writer: he can give a dazzling report (Libedinsky's *The Week*[14] for example) and yet hopelessly falsify, by undertaking to provide this generalization without any perspective. Lacking a perspective of time and place, you must at least keep your mental distance.

And so, for instance, the respect accorded to 'poetry' at the expense of facts and accurate records has encouraged the Rabkor poets to publish a collection called *Petals*,[15] with lines like:

C

> I am a proletarian big gun
> I fire and make 'em run.

There's a lesson to be learnt here: (1) Let's drop all this gibberish about unfurling the 'epic canvas' during a period of war on the barricades – your canvas will be torn to shreds on all sides. (2) The value of factual material (and this is why documentary reports from the workers' and peasants' journalists are so interesting) must be marked at a higher price – and under no circumstances at a lower one – than so-called 'poetical works'. Premature 'poeticization' only emasculates and mangles the material. All textbooks of poetry a là Shengeli are pernicious because they don't educe the poetry from the material, that is, they don't give us the essence of the facts, they don't compress the facts to produce the essential, concentrated economical formulation, but simply impose an old form on a new fact. More often than not the form doesn't fit: either the fact gets lost altogether, like a flea in a pair of trousers – like Radimov's sucking-pigs in those Greek pentameters of his,[16] which would be more suitable for the *Iliad* – or the fact bulges out of its poetical clothes, and becomes ridiculous instead of sublime. That's how Kirillov's poem 'Sailors' looks, for instance, marching along in its threadbare four-stress amphibrachs, bursting at the seams.

A different plane from that in which the action is accomplished, a certain distance, is indispensable. This doesn't mean, of course, that the poet must sit by the sea and wait for fine weather, while time passes. He must urge time on its way. Substitute a change of place for the slow passage of time, and in the space of one day you literally pass over centuries, in imagination.

In the case of slight or rather trivial things, you must and you can accomplish this shift in perspective rtificially; and indeed this happens of its own accord.

It's a good idea to begin writing a poem about the rst of May in November or December, when you eel a desperate need for May.

In order to write about the tenderness of love, take us No. 7 from the Lubyansky Square to Nogin quare.[17] The appalling jolting will serve to throw ato relief for you, better than anything else, the harm of a life transformed. A shake-up is essential, or the purposes of comparison.

Time is also needed to test the value of things ou've already written.

All the poems I've written on urgent matters in noments of great inspiration, which pleased me when d done them, all of them seemed to me next day rivial, ill-considered, one-dimensional. Something lways clamours desperately for revision.

And so, when I've finished something, I lock it up n my desk for a few days, then take it out again, and nmediately see the faults that had escaped me earlier. I'd overdone things.

But of course this doesn't mean that you can do nings only at inopportune moments. No. You must hoose exactly the right moment. I just want to irect poets' attention to the fact that little agita- ional jingles, thought of as very easy, in fact call for he most unremitting work and the most diverse echnical devices to make up for the shortage of ime.

Even in preparing a hasty agitational poem, you nust, for instance, copy it from the manuscript in the vening, not in the morning. Just glancing through it ater, you'll see a lot of things that can easily e corrected. If you copy it out in the morning, he bulk of the blunders will remain. An understand- ng of how to establish distance and organize time and not iambuses and trochees) should be introduced

as the basic rule in any handbook for working poet
that is printed.

That's why I got further with my poem abou
Esenin on the short journey from Lubyansky Passag
to the Tea Marketing Board (I was on the way t
settle my account) than on all my voyagings. Myas
nitsky was a sharp and needful contrast: after th
solitude of hotel rooms, Myasnitsky was packed wit
people; after the silence of the provinces, there wa
the cheerful hubbub of buses, cars and trams; and a
round, as though challenging the old lamplit villages
were the offices of electro-technical firms.[18]

I walk along, waving my arms and mumbling al
most wordlessly, now shortening my steps so as no
to interrupt my mumbling, now mumbling mor
rapidly in time with my steps.

So the rhythm is trimmed and takes shape – an
rhythm is the basis of any poetic work, resoundin
through the whole thing. Gradually individual word
begin to ease themselves free of this dull roar.

Several words just jump away and never com
back, others hold on, wriggle and squirm a doze
times over, until you can't imagine how any wor
will ever stay in its place (this sensation, developin
with experience, is called talent). More often than no
the most important word emerges first: the wor
that most completely conveys the meaning of th
poem, or the word that underlies the rhyme. Th
other words come forward and take up dependen
positions in relation to the most important word
When the fundamentals are already there, one has
sudden sensation that the rhythm is strained: there'
some little syllable or sound missing. You begin t
shape all the words anew, and the work drives you t
distraction. It's like having a tooth crowned. A hun
dred times (or so it seems) the dentist tries a crow
on the tooth, and it's the wrong size; but at last, afte

a hundred attempts, he presses one down, and it fits. The analogy is all the more apposite in my case, because when at last the crown fits, I (quite literally) have tears in my eyes, from pain and relief.

Where this basic dull roar of a rhythm comes from is a mystery. In my case it's all kinds of repetitions in my mind of noises, rocking motions, or in fact of any phenomenon with which I can associate a sound. The sound of the sea, endlessly repeated, can provide my rhythm, or a servant who slams the door every morning, recurring and intertwining with itself, trailing through my consciousness; or even the rotation of the earth, which in my case, as in a shop full of visual aids, gives way to, and inextricably connects with the whistle of a high wind.

This struggle to organize movement, to organize sounds around oneself, discovering their own proper nature, their peculiarities, is one of the most important constants of the work of the poet: laying in rhythmic supplies. I don't know if the rhythm exists outside me or only inside me – more probably inside. But there must be a jolt, to awaken it; in the same way as the sound of a violin, any violin, provokes a buzz in the guts of the piano, in the same way as a bridge sways to and fro and threatens to collapse under the synchronized tread of ants.

Rhythm is the fundamental force, the fundamental energy of verse. You can't explain it, you can only talk about it as you do about magnetism or electricity. Magnetism and electricity are manifestations of energy. The rhythm can be the same in a lot of poems, even in the whole oeuvre of the poet, and still not make his work monotonous, because a rhythm can be so complex, so intricately shaped, that even several long poems won't exhaust its possibilities.

A poet must develop just this feeling for rhythm in himself, and not go learning up other people's

measurements: iambus, trochee or even this apotheo-
sized free verse: rhythm accommodating itself to
some concrete situation, and of any use only for that
concrete situation. So, for example, magnetic energy,
discharged on to a horseshoe, will pick up iron filings,
and you can't use it for anything else.

I know nothing of metre. Only I'm convinced, on
my own account, that to communicate heroic or
majestic sentiments, you must choose long measures
with a large collection of syllables, and for cheerful
sentiments, short ones. For some reason or other I
have associated the former since childhood (from the
age of nine) with:

> As a sacrifice you fell in that fateful struggle ...[19]

and the latter with:

> Let's bid the old world farewell ...[20]

Curious. But, word of honour, that's how it is.

I get my metre by covering this rhythmical roar
with words, words suggested by the aim or purpose
(all the time you ask yourself: is this the word I
want? Who must I read it to? Will it be understood
in the right way? and so on.) – and with words that
are regulated by a highly developed sense of appropri-
ateness by one's abilities and one's talent.

At first the poem to Esenin just rumbled away
something like this:

> Ta-ra-rá/ra rá/ra, ra ra rá/ra rá/
> ra-ra-ree/ra ra ra/ra ra/ra ra ra ra/
> ra-ra-ra/ra-ra ra ra ra ra raree
> ra-ra-ra/ra ra-ra/rara/ra/ra ra

Then the words emerge:

38

You went off ra ra ra ra ra to a world above
It may be you flew ra ra ra ra ra ra.
No loans for you, no women and no pub.
Ra ra ra/ra ra ra ra/sobriety.

I repeat it a dozen times, listening to the first line:

You went off ra ra ra to a world above ... and so
on.

What is that damned 'ra ra ra', and what can I put
in its place? Perhaps I can leave it without any 'ra ra
ra's.

You went off to a world above.

No! I'm reminded at once of some line or other I've
heard:

The poor steed fell down in the field.

What's that horse doing there! This isn't a horse,
this is Esenin. For without those syllables you get
some kind of operatic 'galop', and even 'ra ra ra' is
much more elevated. On no account must 'ra ra ra'
be expunged – the rhythm is right. I begin to try out
some words.

You went off, *Seryozha*, to a world above ...

You went off for ever to a world above ...

You went off, Esenin, to a world above ...

Which of these lines is the best?
They're all rubbish! Why?
The first line is false because of the word 'Ser-
yozha'. I was never that matey with Esenin, and that

39

word is particularly intolerable now, since it brings in with it a mass of other false words, unrelated to me and to our relations: 'thou', 'sweet', 'brother' and so on.

The second line is bad because the words 'for ever' don't need to be there, they're random and put in only for the metre: not only do they not help, explaining nothing, they merely get in the way. Really, what does it mean, this 'for ever'? Did anyone ever die for a trial period? Is there such a thing as death with a period return ticket?

The third line won't do because it's too heavily serious (the aim or purpose is gradually hammering it into my head that this is the failing of all three lines). Why is this seriousness inadmissible? Because it makes it possible to ascribe to me a belief in a life beyond the grave, expressed in Biblical tones – which I don't have; that's one thing, and the other is that this seriousness turns the verse into something funereal, not tendentious, and blurs my aim. That's why I introduce the words 'they say'.

'You went off, they say, to a world above.' The line is written; 'they say', without being openly mocking, subtly undermines the pathos of the line and at the same time eliminates any possible suspicions about the author's belief in all this life-after-death nonsense. The line is written and at once becomes a *donné* which determines the whole quatrain; it must be equivocal, neither dancing at a funeral nor, on the other hand, yielding to the professional mourners. The quatrain must at once be cut in two: two elevated lines, and two conversational, drawn from everyday life, setting each other off by the contrast. So at once, in accordance with my conviction that for a more cheerful line you must cut down the number of syllables, I set to work on the end of the quatrain.

40

You've no loans, no women and no pub
ra ra rá ra ra rá ra rá sobriety.

What's to be done with these lines? How can I cut
them down? 'No women' must be cut out. Why?
Because these women are alive. To name them in this
way, when the larger part of Esenin's lyrics are very
tenderly devoted to them, is tactless. Therefore it's
false, therefore it sounds wrong. We have left:

You've no loans, and no pub.

I try to murmur them to myself: it doesn't work.
These lines are so different from my first version, that
the rhythm hasn't just changed, it's broken and
smashed utterly. I've cut too much out. So what must
be done? There's a syllable missing. This line, break-
ing out of the rhythm, has become false from another
standpoint: the standpoint of meaning. It doesn't
contrast sufficiently, and then piles all the 'loans and
bar-rooms' on Esenin alone, when they should apply
equally to all of us.
How can I make these lines more contrasted and at
the same time more generalized?
I take the speech of the most simple folk:

Nothing under you, nor anything over you (bad
    luck to you)
No loans now, nor pub.

In the most conversational, the most vulgar form,
this would be:

We got nothing under, and nothing over.
We got no loans now, and no pub.

The line is fixed, as regards metre and sense. 'We

41

got' contrasts that much more with the first lines, while the address in the first line, 'You went off', and in the third 'We got no', at once show that the loans and the bars are not put in to belittle Esenin's memory, but as a general phenomenon. This line has given us such an excellent run-up that we can get rid of all the syllables before 'sobriety', and this sobriety comes like the solution to a problem. And so this line wins over even Esenin's devotees, while remaining in essence almost mocking.

The quatrain is basically ready; only one line remains, not filled out by a rhyme.

> You went off, they say, to a world above,
> It may be you flew ra-ra-rá-ra.
> We got no loans now, and no pub –
> Sobriety.

Perhaps it can be left unrhymed? That's impossible. Why? Because without rhyme (understanding the word in a wide sense) poetry falls to pieces.

Rhyme sends you back to the previous line, reminds you of it, and helps all the lines that compose one thought to hold together.

People usually define rhyme as corresponding sounds in the last words of two lines, when the stressed vowel is the same, and the sounds that follow it are more or less identical.

That's what everyone says, but it's nonsense just the same.

Corresponding ends of lines rhyme – that's only one of an infinite number of ways of drawing lines together, and the simplest and most crude, I may add.

You can rhyme the beginnings of lines as well:

The street –
I meet people with dogs more rarely ... and so on.

You can rhyme the end of one line and the beginning of the next.

A menacing rain narrowed the eyes
While I behind the bars stare . . . and so on.

You can rhyme the end of the first line and the end
of the second both at once with the last word of the
third or the fourth line :

Though he loved a scholarly wrangle
He
Knew next to nothing of verse, our Shengeli.

And so on and so forth, ad infinitum.

In my poem it's imperative to find a rhyme for
'sobriety'. The first words that come into my head
will be words like 'propriety', for example :

You went off, they say, to a world above,
It may be you flew ... you'd love the impropriety!
We got no loans now, and no pub –
Sobriety.

Can we leave this rhyme? No. Why? In the first
place because this rhyme is too rich, too transparent
by far. When you say 'impropriety', the rhyme
'sobriety' forces itself on you willy-nilly, and when
you utter it, it doesn't surprise, it doesn't command
attention. That's the fate of almost all words that are
the same part of speech : if you rhyme a verb with a
verb, a noun with a noun, where the roots are the
same, or the inflections, etc. The word 'impropriety'
is bad for another reason : it introduces an element
of mockery already in the first lines, thus weakening
all the later contrast. Perhaps you could make the
job easier for yourself by replacing the word 'sobriety' by some other word that's easier to rhyme, or

43

by not putting 'sobriety' at the end of the line, but filling out the line instead with a few syllables, for instance: 'sobriety, peace'? … In my opinion, you mustn't do this; I always put the most characteristic word at the end of the line and provide a rhyme for it at all costs. As a result my rhyme-schemes are almost always unusual, or at any rate not used by anyone before me, and they aren't in the rhyming dictionary.

The rhymes bind the lines together, so the material of which they're made must be stronger than the material used for the other lines.

Taking the most characteristic sound of the rhyme-word, 'briet', I repeat it to myself over and over again, attentive to all its associations: 'riot', 'iota', 'right', 'righter', 'brighter'. And a good rhyme has been found. An adjective, not a noun: and ceremonious, to boot!

But here's a problem: in the word 'sobriety' that final syllable 'ty' is clearly audible, even though it isn't as important as the 'briet'. What can we do with it? We must introduce analogous letters into the preceding line.

Therefore we must replace the words 'It may be' by 'infinity', with plenty of 'i' sounds and that 'ty', and for the sake of euphony we change 'flew' to 'fly', the 'f … y' echoing and softening the 'i' sounds of 'infinity'.

And here is our final printed version:

> You went off, they say, to a world above.
> Infinity – you fly, and make the stars shine
> brighter …
> We got no loans now, and no pub –
> Sobriety.

Of course, I'm simplifying too much, schematizing

44

and subjecting the work of the poet to the meddling intellect. Naturally, the process of composition is more devious, more intuitive. But just the same, the work goes on essentially according to this pattern.

The first quatrain determines all the rest of the poem. With a quatrain like this in my hands, I can already calculate how many like it I need on a given theme, and how I can distribute them to produce the best effect: the architectonics of the poem.

If the theme is big and complex, I must allocate to it twenty or thirty bricks of this kind, quatrains, sestets, or couplets.

When I've produced almost all these bricks, I begin to size them up, putting them now in one place, now in another, attending carefully to their sounds, and trying to imagine what sort of effect they produce.

After sizing them up and thinking it over, I decide: first of all I must get my listeners interested by any ambiguity, as a consequence of which they can't tell whose side I'm on, thereby taking Esenin away from those people who are using his death to their own ends; I must praise him and vindicate him in a way his devotees never could, 'piling their dull rhymes in funereal mounds'. I must win over the sympathy of my listeners once and for all, pouncing upon all those who vulgarize Esenin's work, the more so since they vulgarize any other work they get hold of – all these Sobinovs, Kogans, who quickly catch the attention of their listeners with facile couplets.[21] Winning over the audience, seizing the right to speak about Esenin's achievements and about his circle, I unexpectedly shunt my listeners towards a conviction that Esenin's end was totally unremarkable, insignificant, and uninteresting: I have rephrased his last words, and given them a meaning opposite to the one he intended.

A scheme of this kind can be represented by a rudimentary little drawing thus:

When you've got the basic building blocks of the quatrain and you've decided on your architectural plan, you can consider that you've done the essential creative work.

The rest consists of relatively easy technical reworking of the poetic artefact.

You have to bring the poem to the highest pitch of expressiveness. One of the most noteworthy vehicles of this expressiveness is the image. Not that essential visionary image which rises up at the beginning of one's work as a first, dim response to the social command. No, I'm talking about the auxiliary images which help this central image to take shape. These images are one of the contemporary methods of poetry, and a movement like Imaginism, for instance, making them instead the goal, has in essence condemned itself to working on just one of poetry's technical components.

There are endless ways of fabricating images.

One of the most primitive ways of making an image is by comparison. My first things, 'A Cloud in Trousers' for example, were entirely based on similes – 'like, like and like' all the time. Isn't it just this primitive quality that makes later critics consider my 'Cloud' my 'ultimate synthesis' in poetry? In my most recent things and in my 'Esenin', of course, I've got rid of this primitivism. I've discovered only one comparison:

'Drawn-out and boring like Doronin's attempts.'[22]

Why like Doronin, and not like the distance to the moon, for example? In the first place, a comparison drawn from literary life because my whole subject literary. And in the second place, 'The Ploughman of Steel' (is that what it's called?) is longer than the journey to the moon, because that journey is unreal, and 'The Ploughman of Steel' is, alas, real; then the journey to the moon would seem shorter because of its novelty, while Doronin's four thousand lines afflict you with the monotony of a verbal and metrical landscape you've seen sixteen thousand times before. And then of course the image must be tendentious, that is, elaborating a large subject, and you must use separate little images that you come across along the way to help in the struggle, in your literary agitation.

The most commonly accepted way of making images is by the use of metaphor, that is, by transferring attributes, which up to the present have been associated with certain things only, to other words, things, phenomena and notions.

For instance the metaphorical line:

And they bear funereal scraps of verse.

We've heard of scrap-iron, and of table-scraps. But how are we to describe those odds and ends of poetry, left over otiosely, which can't be made use of anywhere else when they've been part of other poems already? These, of course, are scrap verse, or verse-scraps. And in this case, the scrap is all of one kind — funereal, these are funereal verse-scraps. We can't have the line like that, because we get 'verse-scraps', which, when you read it, sounds like 'verse-crap', and there's what we might call a 'shift in meaning' which ruins the line from the point of view of the sense. That kind of carelessness is very common.

For example in a lyrical poem of Utkin's[23] printe
not long ago in the journal *Projector* there are th
lines:

He comes again no more, ah
So the swan comes not when lakes freeze hard
as glass.

You can distinctly hear the word 'arse'.
The first line of a poem published by Bryusov i
the early days of the war, in the journal *Ou
Times*,[24] is particularly effective:

We were a regiment who learnt what danger mean

The shift in meaning is disposed of if you give
simpler, more telling order to the words –

funereal scraps of verse

One way of making an image, the one I've most o
all adopted recently, is by describing the most fa
tastic events and facts, reinforced by exaggeration.

So that Kogan scattered that way and this
Impaling passers-by on his moustache's bayonets.

In this way Kogan becomes a collectivity, whic
allows him to run in all directions, his moustach
turn into bayonets, and to intensify the idea o
bayonets people lie around, run through by his mou
taches.
Ways of forming images vary, like all the other d
vices of poetry, according to how familiar or ove
familiar the reader is with one form or another.
You can have imagery on the opposite principl
such that it not only doesn't enlarge the scope o

what's said, by means of the imagination, but on the contrary tries to squeeze the impression made by the words into a deliberately limited framework. For example, in my old poem 'War and the Universe':

> In the rotting waggon were forty men –
> But only four legs.

Many of Selvinsky's[25] things are based on numerical images of this kind.

After that comes the work of selecting your verbal material. You have to take accurate stock of the milieu in which your poetical work is being carried on, so that no word foreign to these conditions can get in by accident.

For example, I had the line:

What things, my dear friend, you knew of.

'My dear friend' is false, firstly because it goes clean against the stern, accusatory development of the poem; secondly because we have never used this locution in our poetic circles. Thirdly, it's petty, and often employed in meaningless conversations, and used more often to suppress feelings than to show them more clearly. Fourthly, a man who is truly moved by grief will find a much harsher word to take refuge behind. In any case, this word doesn't specify *what* the man knew of – *what* did you know of, Esenin?

What did Esenin know? There's a big demand for his verse now, and endless rapt attention to his lyrics; Esenin's literary progress has been governed by so-called literary scandal (not something shameful, but treated with great respect, as an echo of the comparable fate of the famous Futurist performances) and these scandals were really literary landmarks, milestones, for Esenin, during his lifetime.

D

How inapposite it would have been while he was alive:

What things you could sing of to our souls.

Esenin wasn't a singer (fundamentally, of course, he was a gypsy guitar-player, but he was saved as a poet by the fact that as long as he lived, at any rate, he wasn't taken for one, and in his volumes there are a dozen genuinely poetical innovations). Esenin didn't sing, he shouted abuse, he played the hooligan. I used *that* expression only after a lot of thought, and regardless of how much such a word may annoy the nurslings of the literary brothels, who listen to wild abuse all day, while they dream poetically of their souls inhabiting lilac, of bosoms, the warbling of nightingales, soft harmonies and flushed cheeks.

Without any comment at all I'll record the gradual revision of the words of one line:

1. Our days are ill-equipped for merriment.
2. Our days are ill-equipped for joy.
3. Our days are ill-equipped for happiness.
4. Our life is ill-equipped for merriment.
5. Our life is ill-equipped for joy.
6. Our life is ill-equipped for happiness.
7. For revels our planet is ill-equipped.
8. For gaiety our planet is ill-equipped.
9. Not specially well is our planet equipped for revels.
10. Not specially well is our planet equipped for merriment.
11. Our little planet for pleasures is ill-equipped.

and finally, the last, the twelfth:

12. For merriment our planet isn't well equipped.

I could deliver a whole speech for the defence, on behalf of the last of these lines, but I'll content myself for the moment with simply copying these lines from the manuscript so as to demonstrate how much work you must put in just to choose a few words.

The sound quality of the thing is connected with this technical revision; the way one word combines with another. This is the 'magic of words', this is why perhaps everything in life is just a means to create sonorous and melodious verses',[26] this musical aspect seems to many people a poetic end in itself, but again it brings us back to the level of technical work. Overdoing assonance, alliteration and so on, produces an impression of satiety after only a short time.

For example Balmont :

> I, the wild wind, woefully wail,
> Whip up the waves ... and so on.[27]

Doses of alliteration must be administered with extreme caution and as far as possible the repetitions mustn't be obvious. An example of clear alliteration in my Esenin poem is the line :

Where is it, the sounding bronze or the grey granite?

I have recourse to alliteration to provide a framework for, or to emphasize more strongly, words that are important to me. It's possible to have recourse to alliteration just to play with words, as a poetic pastime; old poets (old to us) used alliteration largely for its melodic effect, or verbal music, and thus often made use of a kind of sound harmony that to me is usually hateful – onomatopoeia. I've already spoken of the different kinds of alliteration in speaking about rhyme.

Of course, it's not obligatory to garnish poems with alliteration of an affected kind and make them

51

unheard-of masses of rhyme. You must always re-member that a policy of economy in art is the most important principle of every product of aesthetic value. For this reason, when you've done the basic work I spoke of earlier, you must suppress many passages of fine writing, and many fine fancies, to gain brilliancy in other places.

You can, for example, half rhyme lines, connecting one word that doesn't at once catch the ear with an other, to lead up to a dazzling and thunderous rhyme

And this once again underlines the relativity of all rules about writing verse.

The question of the tone of a poetic work is connected with matters of technique.

You mustn't design the thing to function in some airless nothingness, or, as is often the case with poetry, in an all too airy nothingness.

You must keep your audience constantly in front of your eyes, the audience to whom this poem is directed. This is particularly important in our day when the most significant means of communicating with the masses is the auditorium, the public platform, the voice, the spoken word.

You must adopt a tone that fits your audience – persuasive or pleading, commanding or questioning.

The larger part of my things are based on a conversational tone. But despite all my careful planning this tone isn't a fixed thing, established once for all, but a stance that I quite often change in the course of reading, according to the kind of audience I have. Thus for example the printed text speaks in rather dispassionate tones, aiming at a qualified reader :

One must tear happiness from the days to come.

Sometimes on the lecture platform I intensify this line until it's a shout.

A slogan:

> tear happiness from the days to come!

So you mustn't be surprised if you come across a poem reproduced by someone in its printed form, and the disposition of the words carries a slightly different emphasis in different versions.

When you're writing a poem that's destined for publication, you must calculate how the printed text will be received *as* a printed text. You must take the reader's reactions into account, and direct his attention by every possible means to exactly that form which you as a writer wanted to give your line of poetry. Our accepted system of punctuation, with full stops, commas, and question and exclamation marks is extremely poor and inexpressive compared with those nuances of feeling with which a complex human being can invest a poetical work.

Metre and rhythm are more significant than punctuation, and they bend punctuation to their will when it follows established patterns.

For instance, everybody reads Alexey Tolstoy's lines

> Shibanov was silent. From his pierced leg
> Blood streamed in a red jet ...[28]

as —

> Shibanov was silent from his pierced leg ...

And again ...

> Begone, rather. Ashamed I am
> To cringe before the proud Pole ...[29]

reads like some suburban chatter

Begone. Rather ashamed I am ...

To read it as Pushkin intended, you must divide up
the line as I divide it:

> Begone rather;
>> ashamed I am ...

Divided this way into two hemistichs there will be
no confusion in either the sense or the rhythm. The
way lines are divided is often dictated by the neces-
sity of hammering home the rhythm unmistakably,
since our condensed and economical verse-forms often
oblige us to discard intervening words and syllables,
and if you don't make a pause after these syllables
and often a bigger pause than between lines, the
rhythm is cut off in mid-air.

That's why I write:

> Infinity ...
>> You fly
>>> and make the stars shine brighter.

'Infinity' stands apart, a word on its own, charac-
terizing the landscape of the heavens. 'You fly' stands
apart, to avoid it sounding like an imperative ('Fly
and make the stars ...') and so on.

One of the crucial moments in a poem, especially
when it's tendentious and declamatory, is its ending.
The most effective lines of the poem usually come
in this last bit. Sometimes you refashion the whole
poem simply in order to justify such a rearrangement.

A paraphrase of Esenin's last lines was an obvious
way of concluding the poem.

They sound like this:

Esenin's –

> In this life it's nothing new to die
> But to live, of course, isn't newer.

Mine –

> In this life to die has never been hard.
> To make new life's more difficult by far.

Throughout all my work on the whole poem I kept these lines in mind constantly. Working on other lines, I came back all the time to these – consciously or unconsciously.

It was quite impossible to forget what I had to do here, so I didn't write these lines down, but kept them in my head (as I formerly did with all my poems, and still do with the most hard-hitting ones).

So it isn't possible to calculate how many revisions I made but at all events there were no fewer than fifty or sixty variants of these two lines.

There are countless different technical devices you can use in fashioning words, and it's useless to talk about them, since the essence of poetic activity, as I've mentioned here more than once, lies precisely in the very ability to invent these devices, and they are what makes a writer a professional. The high priests of poetry will, I'm sure, pull long faces over this book of mine, since they love to proffer ready-made formulas for poetry. You take a certain theme, cover it in a poetic form, iambuses or trochees, rhyme the ends, add a little alliteration, fill it up with images – and your poem is ready.

But in every publishing house they chuck this kind of patchwork straight into the wastepaper-basket, and it's a good thing that they do.

A man who has just got hold of a pen for the first time, and wants to write poetry after a week, won't find my book much use.

My book will be useful to a man who, despite all the obstacles, wants to be a poet; a man who, knowing that poetry is one of the most difficult things to manufacture, wants to master and to pass on some of what seem the most mysterious techniques of this productive process.

Some conclusions:

1. Poetry is a manufacture. A very difficult, very complex kind, but a manufacture.

2. Instruction in poetical work doesn't consist of the study of already fixed and delimited models of poetical works, but a study of the procedures of manufacture, a study that helps us to make new things.

3. Innovation, innovation in materials and methods, is obligatory for every poetical composition.

4. The work of the verse-maker must be carried on daily, to perfect his craft, and to lay in poetical supplies.

5. A good notebook and an understanding of how to make use of it are more important than knowing how to write faultlessly in worn-out metres.

6. Don't set in motion a huge poetry factory just to make poetic cigarette lighters. You must renounce the uneconomical production of poetical trifles. Reach for your pen only when there is no other way of saying something except verse. You must work up things you've prepared only when you feel a clear social command.

7. To understand the social command accurately, a poet must be in the middle of things and events. A knowledge of theoretical economics, a knowledge of the realities of everyday life, an immersion in the scientific study of history are for the poet, in the very fundamentals of his work, more important than scholarly textbooks by idealist professors who worship the past.

8. To fulfil the social command as well as possible you must be in the vanguard of your class, and carry on the struggle, along with your class, on all fronts. You must smash to smithereens the myth of an

56

political art. This old myth is appearing again now in new form under cover of twaddle about 'broad epic canvases' (first epic, then objective, and in the end politically uncommitted), or about the 'grand style' (first grand, then elevated, and in the end celestial) and so on and so forth.

9. Only by approaching art as a manufacture can you eliminate chance, arbitrariness of taste and subjectivity of values. Only by regarding it as a manufacture can you get the different aspects of literary work in perspective : poems, and reports by workers' and peasants' journalists. Instead of mystically pondering a poetic theme you will have the power to tackle a pressing problem with accuracy, by means of poetic tariffs and standards.

10. You mustn't make the manufacturing, the so-called technical process, an end in itself. But it *is* this process of manufacture that makes the poetic work fit for use. It's the difference just in these methods of production that marks the difference between poets, and only a knowledge, a mastery, an accumulation of the widest possible range of varied literary devices makes a man a professional writer.

11. The everyday circumstances of poetry have as much influence on the composition of a real work of art as other factors do. The word 'Bohemian' has become a term of opprobrium describing every artistic-Philistine way of life. Unfortunately war has often been waged on the *word* 'Bohemian', and only on the word. But what remains actively with us is the individualist and careerist atmosphere of the old literary world, the petty interests of malevolent coteries, mutual back-scratching; and the word 'poetical' has come to mean 'lax', 'a bit drunk', 'debauched' and so on. Even the way a poet dresses and the way he talks to his wife at home has to be different, and entirely dictated by the kind of poetry

he writes.

12. We, the poets of the Left Front,[30] never clai
that we alone possess the secrets of poetical crea
ivity. But we are the only ones who want to la
these secrets open, the only ones who don't want t
surround the creative process with a catchpenn
religio-artistic aura of sanctity.

My undertaking here is the feeble undertaking c
just one man, making use of the theoretical work c
my fellow students of literature.

These students of literature must bring their wor
to bear on contemporary material and give their hel
freely to the poetry of the future.

But this is not enough.

The organs of mass education must shake the teac
ing of the old aesthetics to its very foundations.

Sergey Esenin   the farewell poem   (1925)

Goodbye, my friend, goodbye.
Dear friend, you live in my heart.
Although we were fated to part
We are fated to meet bye and bye.

Goodbye, my friend, without handshakes, without
    murmur,
Don't be sad, why such grief in your eye?
In this life it's nothing new to die,
But to live, of course, isn't newer.

To Sergey Esenin   (1926)

You went off,
>   they say,
>   to a world above.
Infinity –
>   You fly,
>   and make the stars shine brighter.
We got no loans now,
>   and no pub
Sobriety.
No, Esenin,
>   I
>   don't want to gloat.
I see how
>   you linger with your cut wrists
And with grief
>   not laughter
>   sticking in my throat
See the sack
>   of your own bones
>   that you hoist.
– Cut it out!
>   Drop it!
>   You gone mad or something?
Making death
>   pour
>   over your cheeks
>   like chalk?
You of all people
>   who to death
>   could bring
Like no one else
>   on earth
>   your swaggering talk.

60

СЕРГЕЮ ЕСЕНИНУ

Вы ушли,
          как говорится,
                         в мир иной.
Пустота...
          Летите,
                   в звезды врезываясь.
Ни тебе аванса,
                ни пивной.
Трезвость.
Нет, Есенин,
            это
                не насмешка.
В горле
        горе комом —
                       не смешок.
Вижу —
        взрезанной рукой помешкав,
собственных
             костей
                    качаете мешок.
— Прекратите!
              Бросьте!
                       Вы в своем уме ли?
Дать,
      чтоб щеки
                заливал
                         смертельный мел?!
Вы ж
     такое
           загибать умели,
что другой
           на свете
                     не умел.

61

Why?
        For what cause?
                        Bewilderment dumbs me.
The critics mutter :
                    – The trouble was, we find
This ...
        or that ...
                    but chiefly anomy,
The result of
            too much beer or wine.
In other words
            if you'd swapped
                            Bohemia
                                    for the work
                                        ing class
Class-conscious, you
                    wouldn't have come to this.
But do the workers
                drink
                        nothing stronger than kvass.
That class, too,
            enjoys getting pissed.
In other words
            if a Party man
                        had been given the chore
Of watching
            that your main stress
                            was on content,
You'd have written
                every day
                            lines
                                by the score
Drawn-out
        and boring
                like Doronin's attempts.
But in my view
            if you'd known that kind of delirium
62

Почему?

Зачем?

Недоуменье смяло.

Критики бормочут:

— Этому вина

то...

да сё...

а главное,

что смычки мало,

в результате

много пива и вина. —

Дескать,

заменить бы вам

богему

классом,

класс влиял на вас,

и было б не до драк.

Ну, а класс-то

жажду

заливает квасом?

Класс — он тоже

выпить не дурак.

Дескать,

к вам приставить бы

кого из напостов —

стали б

содержанием

премного одарённей.

Вы бы

в день

писали

строк по сто,

утомительно

и длинно,

как Доронин.

А по-моему,

осуществись

такая бредь,

You'd have laid
                    hands on yourself
                              much earlier on.
Better die of vodka
                    in my opinion
Than of boredom!
They'll never tell us
                    the cause
                              of our loss,
That noose
          there, or that penknife.
But if there'd been
                    ink
                         in the Angleterre, of course,
You needn't have cut
                    your veins
                              when you took your
                                        life.
Your imitators were delighted:
                              encore!
A platoon, almost,
                    laid hands
                         wildly on themselves.
Why make
          the number
                    of suicides more?
Better supply
          ink
                    to all our hotels!
For ever
          now
                    your tongue
                              's locked behind your teeth
It's pedantic
          and misplaced
                    riddling like this.

на себя бы
          раньше наложили руки.

Лучше уж
          от водки умереть,
чем от скуки!
Не откроют
          нам
               причин потери
ни петля,
          ни ножик перочинный.
Может,
     окажись
               чернила в «Англетере»,
вены
     резать
          не было б причины.

Подражатели обрадовались:
                              бис!
Над собою
          чуть не взвод
                         расправу учинил.
Почему же
          увеличивать
                    число самоубийств?
Лучше
     увеличь
          изготовление чернил!
Навсегда
     теперь
          язык
               в зубах затворится.
Тяжело
     и неуместно
               разводить мистерии.

E   65

The people,
            in whom our language lives and breathes
Have lost in death
                their sonorous
                                debauchee-'prentice
And they bear
            funereal scraps of verse
From past
        burials,
                with hardly a revision.
Piling
    their dull rhymes
                        in funereal mounds : worse
Than useless
            to honour
                    the Muses' son.
For you
        a monument
                    is not cast yet.
Where is it,
            the sounding bronze
                                or the grey granite ?
But by the railings
                of the monument
                                    they've already set
Down rubbish,
            dedications, reminiscences, all shit.
Your name
        is snivelled into handkerchiefs.
Your words
            are slobbered by Sobinov
And he winds up
                under a droopy birch-tree –
'Not one word,
            o my friend,
                        nor si-i-igh let there be.'

У народа,
          у языкотворца,
умер
     звонкий
                забулдыга подмастерье.
И несут
        стихов заупокойный лом,
с прошлых
          с похорон
                     не переделавши почти.
В холм
       тупые рифмы
                   загонять колом —
разве так
          поэта
               надо бы почтить ?
Вам
   и памятник еще не слит, —

где он,
        бронзы звон
                    или гранита грань ? —
а к решеткам памяти
                     уже
                         понанесли
посвящений
           и воспоминаний дрянь.
Ваше имя
         в платочки рассоплено,
ваше слово
          слюнявит Собинов
и выводит
          под березкой дохлой —
«Ни слова,
           о дру-уг мой,
                         ни вздо-о-о-о-ха».

Agh,
    you'd have set about him with great glee,
This goddamn
            Leonid Lohengrinsky!
You'd have set up
            a thunderous row
'I won't permit
            poetic burblings
                        from braying asses.' —
And you'd deafen them
            tridactylously
                    whistling, now
And tell them
            they could stuff it up their arses.
To send packing all
            these talentless shits,
Filling
    the black sails
            of their smoking-jackets,
So that Kogan
        scattered,
                that way and this,
Impaling passers-by
            on his moustaches'
                        bayonets.
These shits
        meanwhile
                haven't grown any fewer.
It's a big job
        just to catch them up.
Life
    must be
            started quite anew,
When you've changed it
                then the singing can start up.

68

Эх,
    поговорить бы и́наче
с этим самым
                с Леонидом Лоэнгринычем!
Встать бы здесь
                гремящим скандалистом:
— Не позволю
        мямлить стих
                    и мять! —
Оглушить бы
        их
            трехпалым свистом
в бабушку
        и в бога душу мать!
Чтобы разнеслась
                бездарнейшая погань,
раздувая
    темь
        пиджачных парусов,
чтобы
    врассыпную
                разбежался Коган,
встреченных
            увеча
                пиками усов.
Дрянь
    пока что
            мало поредела.
Дела много —
            только поспевать.
Надо
    жизнь
        сначала переделать,
переделав —
            можно воспевать.

69

Such an age
            poses problems
                        for the pen,
But show me
            you feeble
                        bunch of cripples
Where some great man
            has chosen,
                        and when,
To follow
            a path of roses, not of thistles?
Words are
            the commanders
                        of mankind's forces.
March!
            And behind us
                        time
                                    explodes like a land-mine
To the past
            we offer
                        only the streaming tresses
Of our hair
            tangled
                        by the wind.
For merriment
            our planet
                        isn't well equipped.
One must
            tear
                        happiness
                                    from the days to come.
In this life
            to die
                        has never been hard.
To make new life
                        's more difficult
                                    by far.

Это время —
            трудновато для пера,

но скажите
            вы,
                калеки и калекши,
где,
    когда,
            какой великий выбирал
путь,
    чтобы протоптанней
                        и легше?
Слово —
        полководец
                    человечьей силы.
Марш!
    Чтоб время
                сзади
                        ядрами рвалось.
К старым дням
            чтоб ветром
                        относило
только
    путаницу волос.

Для веселия
            планета наша
                        мало оборудована.
Надо
    вырвать
            радость
                    у грядущих дней.
В этой жизни
            помереть
                    не трудно.
Сделать жизнь
            значительно трудней.

NOTES

1 The most progressive writers in Russia formed, after the Revolution, associations which were known as Associations of Proletarian Writers (in Russian the initial letters would be A.P.P.). There was, for instance, MAPP, the Moscow association, formed in 1923; and RAPP, the Russian Association, which took over from VAPP, the ALL-Russian Association. Mayakovsky loved these neologisms.

2 The Formalists: two schools of literary critics active in the 'twenties, one in Leningrad, the other in Moscow, concerned with analysing the language of literature and the devices used by writers. Mayakovsky admired their work and was a close friend of one of the most talented members of the Moscow group, Osip Brik. At this time 'Formalist' had not yet become a term of abuse.

3 The principal characters in Pushkin's novel in verse *Evgeny Oniegin*. Alexander Sergeyevich Pushkin (1799–1837) was the greatest Romantic poet of Russia. *Eugene Oniegin* (finished in 1830) superficially influenced by Byron, was extremely influential in the literature of the nineteenth century.

4 References to specific lines in Pushkin's poem (Chapter One).

5 Georgy Arkadievich Shengeli (1894–1956), poet and literary theorist, published a short book in 1926 called *How to Write Articles, Verses, and Stories*, intended primarily to help workers produce more literate wall newspapers. Shengeli comes out with remarks like: 'One single metre is usually chosen for a poem; a mixture of metres, with the first line an iambus, the second a dactyl and so on, is inadmissible.' Mayakovsky's essay was written as a reply to this: the *Kak pisat' ... stikhi* of Shengeli's title prompted the *Kak delat' stikhi* of Mayakovsky's. Shengeli then replied with a booklet called *Mayakovsky vo ves' rost*, or *Mayakovsky full length* (either vertically or horizontally). Mayakovsky was un usually tall.

6 Nikolay Ivanovich Lobachevsky (1793–1856), a Russian mathematician.

72

7 Philologists: Nikolay Grech's textbook was published in 1820, Abramov's *Rhyming Dictionary* in 1912.
8 Mayakovsky quotes (inaccurately) from a poem of Zinaida Gippius (1869–1945) called 'One Moment', published in a collection of 1918.
9 Vladimir Timofeyevich Kirillov (1889–1943) published his poem 'To Sailors' on the first anniversary of the Revolution.
10 From the famous revolutionary poem by Alexander Blok (1881–1921) 'The Twelve'.
11 From Mayakovsky's poem 'Left March' (1918).
12 Also from 'The Twelve'.
13 A street-ballad couplet that Mayakovsky composed in 1917, based on the reported shout of the sailors who stormed the Winter Palace.
14 Urban ballads or jingles of just this kind.
15 A term coined by Trotsky (*Literature and Revolution*) whose meaning was subsequently enlarged to include all those writers who were not Communists, but were to some degree sympathetic to the Soviet cause. In the 'twenties it was still possible to discuss their work objectively.
16 The first line of a lyric by Michael Yurievich Lermontov (1814–1841).
17 A specific reference to Shengeli's book.
18 The White general N. N. Yudenich unsuccessfully attacked Petersburg in 1919.
19 Demyan Bedny (it means Demyan the Poor) was the pseudonym of the Soviet poet Efim Alexeyevich Pridvorov (1883–1945), an early Bolshevik and effective publicist.
20 Alexey Eliseyevich Kruchënikh (1886–) was a Futurist colleague of Mayakovsky's. His poetry became gradually more and more experimental, sheer sound, until it was close to Dada.
21 The Communist International.
22 The *Nauchnaya Organizatsiya Truda*, or Scientific Organization of Labour, was set up in order to supply factories with information and equipment to promote their more scientific and efficient running.
23 Part of Mayakovsky's early masterpiece, 'The Cloud in Trousers', a love poem published in 1915.
24 One of many similar dilettante-literary pre-revolutionary journals. This one was a supplement to *Moskovsky Listok*.

25 From Pasternak's poem 'Marburg'. Boris Pasternak (1890–1960) was associated with LEF (the Left Front in Art) and admired Mayakovsky's earlier poetry, especially 'The Cloud in Trousers'. He went to Marburg to hear the lectures of Hermann Cohen before the First World War. The poem was first published in the collection *Across Barriers* (1917). Mayakovsky (as so often) misquotes.

CHAPTER 2

1 Nikolay Alexeyevich Kluyev (1887–1937) was a peasant poet who at first supported the Revolution in the name of the peasants. But his idealized notions of the soil were at odds with Soviet collectivization, and after the late 'twenties his poetry was not published. He died in a labour camp.

2 Maxim Gorky (1868–1936) left Russia in 1921 but, after some years in Berlin and Capri, returned (1928). He occupied a highly influential position in Soviet society and did a lot to help young writers. His sentimental-realist novels strongly influenced many Soviet novelists and were often taken as a model of 'Socialist Realism', the official literary philosophy formulated in the 'thirties.

3 Imaginism was a post-Revolutionary literary movement which would count for little in the history of Russian poetry if it were not for Esenin's association with it. Taking some notions, at several removes, from the Imagist poets of the West, they insisted on the primary importance of the Image in poetry: for Esenin this meant primarily the creation of sensuously beautiful pictures.

4 The All-Russian Association of Proletarian Writers (1925–28).

5 Nikolay Aseyev (1889–) was a Futurist poet, and the close friend and ardent disciple of Mayakovsky.

6 Esenin committed suicide on December 27th, 1925 in the Hotel Angleterre in Leningrad, by cutting his wrists and then hanging himself. He left a farewell poem, written in his blood, the last lines of which gave Mayakovsky the starting point for his poem 'To Sergey Esenin'.

7 Alexander Ilich Bezimensky (1898), the proletarian poet, wrote a poem entitled 'Meeting with Esenin', which began 'Seryozha! My dear friend!' Mayakovsky regards this familiar form of Esenin's name as particularly unsuitable for a poet who was not one of the Esenin circle.

8 Alexander Zharov (1904) published a poem (January

10th, 1926) entitled 'On Esenin's Coffin', which contains these lines.

9 Pyotr Semyonovich Kogan (1872–1932), President of the Moscow Academy of Arts, wrote a number of laudatory articles on Esenin.

10 Luka is a saintly fool in Gorky's play *The Lower Depths*. Mayakovsky has misquoted the line.

11 Kruchënikh published several booklets on Esenin in 1926, of an offensively hostile kind.

12 The New Economic Policy, or NEP, was in force from 1921 to 1929. It involved a relaxing of economic rigour as some private enterprise was encouraged in an attempt to restore the country's economy to a healthy condition after the devastation of the Civil War period. Mayakovsky hated it, and where private and State enterprise were in competition, gave his support wholeheartedly to the State, and against what he saw as the survival and even revival of the old social order.

13 *Na Postu*, On Guard, and hence *Napostov*, those Proletarian contributors to the journal of that title, which followed a rigid and at bottom Philistine line.

14 Yury Libedinsky (1898–) became famous through his novel *The Week* (1922). In it he tried to give a sense of the flux and confusion of the Civil War, but drew general conclusions which Mayakovsky thought premature.

15 *Petals* was a literary collection by the worker-correspondents (Rabkor) from the Khamovnichesky district, published in 1924. The lines cited are from a play called *Carmagnole* by Elmar Grin (1909–).

16 Pavel Alexandrovich Radimov (1887–) published (1926) a collection of poems in hexameters entitled *The Waggon*. Mayakovsky is referring specifically to the poem entitled 'A herd of pigs'.

17 Lubyansky Square is now Dzerzhinsky Square.

18 Mayakovsky had a study in Lubyansky Passage (now Serov Passage). Myasnitsky is now Kirov St.

19 A line from 'a Revolutionary Funeral March'.

20 A popular revolutionary song from the days of the Narodniki (the Russian Populists). It was written in 1875 by Peter Lavrov.

21 Leonid Vitalyevich Sobinov was a tenor with the Bolshoi Opera. Mayakovsky found his participation in a sentimental commemorative evening for Esenin at the Moscow Art Theatre, when he sang settings of some poems of Esenin's, offensive, and an insult to Esenin's poetry.

22 Ivan Ivanovich Doronin (1900–) published in 1926 a poem called not 'The Ploughman of Steel' but 'The Tractor Ploughman'.
23 Iosif Utkin (1903–1944) published in 1926 a poem called 'The Burial Mound', from which these lines are taken.
24 Mayakovsky here misquotes from a translation by Bryusov of Verhaeren's poem 'Pestilence'. Emile Verhaeren, the Belgian poet, was born in 1855 and died in 1916.
25 Ilya Lvovich Selvinsky (1899–), a Constructivist poet whose work is full of technical terminology.
26 Mayakovsky here refers to a line from Valery Yakovlevich Bryusov's poem 'To the Poet', though the notion seems to originate with Mallarmé. Bryusov was born in 1873 and died in 1924.
27 From the poem entitled 'Snowflowers' by Konstantin Dmitrievich Balmont (1867–1942).
28 From the ballad 'Vassily Shibanov' by Alexey Konstantinovich Tolstoy (1817–1875).
29 From Pushkin's verse drama *Boris Godunov*.
30 Left Front: in 1923 Mayakovsky founded and edited the journal *LEF* (*The Left Front in Art*), and later *Novy LEF*, its successor. It was the journal of the Futurists, claiming for them the first place in the art of the future, committed to radical experimentation, and strongly opposed to realism. It soon ran into ideological opposition.

SELECTED BIBLIOGRAPHY

A list of the principal works of Vladimir Mayakovsky with the dates of their first appearance

VLADIMIR MAYAKOVSKY – A Tragedy (play) (*Russian Futurists*, Moscow, 1914)

OBLAKO V. SHTANAKH ('The Cloud in Trousers') (Asis, Petrograd, 1915)

FLEYTA-POZVONOCHNIK ('The Backbone Flute') (Vzyal, Petrograd, 1916)

VOYNA I MIR ('War and the Universe') (Parus, Petrograd, 1917)

MISTERIYA-BUFF ('Mystery-Bouffe') (play) (Svoboda, Petrograd, 1918)

150,000,000 (Giz, Moscow, 1921)

LYUBLYU ('I love') (Vkhutemas, Moscow, 1922)

PRO ETO ('About this') (Giz, Petrograd, 1923)

VLADIMIR ILYICH LENIN (Giz, Moscow, 1925)

SERGEYU ESENINU ('To Sergey Esenin') (Zakkniga, Tiflis, 1926)

KAK DELAT' STIKHI? ('How are verses made?') (Novy Mir, 1926; Ogonyok, Moscow, 1927)

KHOROSHO! ('O.K!') (Giz, Leningrad, 1927)

KLOP ('The Bedbug') (play) (Iskusstvo, Moscow, 1954 – written 1928–9)

BANYA ('The Bath House') (play) (Giz, Moscow–Leningrad, 1930)

VO VES' GOLOS ('At the top of my voice') (Moskovsky Rabochy, Moscow, 1930)

Principal Russian editions of Mayakovsky's collected works

POLNOYE SOBRANIYE SOCHINENII, edited by L. Y. Brik

and I. Bespolav, 12 vols (Goslitizdat, Moscow 1934–8)

POLNOYE SOBRANIYE SOCHINENII, edited by N. Aseyev L. V. Mayakovskaya, V. O. Pertsov and M. N Serebryansky, 12 vols (Goslitizdat, Moscow 1939–49)

POLNOYE SOBRANIYE SOCHINENII, edited by V. A Katanyan, 12 vols (Gos. Izd. Khud. Lit., Moscow 1955–61)

Principal English translations of Mayakovsky's works

Hayward and Reavey (trs), Patricia Blake (ed.), *The Bedbug and Selected Poetry* (Weidenfeld and Nicolson, London, 1961)

Lindsay, Jack, *Russian Poetry 1917–1955* (Bodley Head, London, 1957)

Marshall, Herbert, *Mayakovsky* (Dobson, London, 1965) (the definitive English translation of the poetry)

Marshall, Herbert, *Mayakovsky and his poetry* (Bombay, 1955; Pilot Press, London, n.d.)

Noyes, G. R., *Masterpieces of the Russian Drama*, a two-volume anthology (Dover Books, New York, 1961)

Obolensky, Dmitri, *The Penguin Book of Russian Verse* (Penguin Books, Harmondsworth, 1962)

Reavey and Slonim, *Soviet Literature*, an anthology (Wishart, London, 1933)

THE AUTHOR

Vladimir Vladimirovich Mayakovsky was born in Bagdadi (now Mayakovsky), Georgia, in 1883. Son of a forester, he moved with his family to Moscow after his father's death in 1906; when still in his teens he became actively involved in revolutionary politics, and was imprisoned three times. He studied at the Moscow Training College of Painting and Fine Arts, where he met the poet and artist David Burlyuk, who encouraged him to be a poet. In 1910 the Futurist group was formed, and Mayakovsky soon came to play the leading part in it. After his expulsion from the Art College in 1914, he gave an exhibition of his paintings, and his poetry was highly praised by Gorky. He dedicated his talents wholeheartedly to the Revolution, and worked for the Russian Telegraph Agency during the Civil War, producing propaganda poems and posters of a high artistic order. After the introduction of the New Economic Policy, to which Mayakovsky was largely hostile, his poetry concerned itself more and more frequently with attacks on bureaucracy and the resurgent bourgeoisie; along with which he wrote agitational poems and slogans on behalf of state-run commercial enterprises, which were during that period in competition with private enterprise. In 1923 he helped found the Futurist review *LEF*. He gave lecture tours throughout the Soviet Union, as well as in America. *LEF* ceased publication in 1925, and the successor to it, called *New LEF*, which Mayakovsky founded in 1927, soon ran into strong opposition from the conservatives. His play *The Bath House*, produced in Leningrad in 1930, was a failure, and shortly after it had been mounted in Moscow with the same lack of success, Mayakovsky shot himself (April 14th, 1930).

79